I Remember
Hill Lodge, Freshwater

Memories of
Ellen Victoria Jane Stevenson 1892–1992

Produced by
Freshwater & Totland Archive Group

www.beachybooks.com

First published by Beachy Books in 2017
www.beachybooks.com

1 2 3 4 5 6 7 8 9 10

© Freshwater & Totland Archive Group 2017.

The right of Freshwater & Totland Archive Group to be identified as the Author of this work has been asserted in accordance with the Copyrights, Designs and Patents Act 1988.

British Library Cataloguing in Publication Data.
A catalogue record for this book is available from the British Library.

ISBN: 9780956298096

Design and typesetting by Philip Bell (Beachy Books)

Set in Palatino

Contents

Acknowledgements

Compiled by Pauline Tyrell and Caroline Dudley from material donated to Freshwater & Totland Archive Group.

Ellen's journals are reproduced with the full permission of her family to whom we are grateful for images and biographical information. Many thanks especially to Vicki Knopf, Bonnie Huntsinger and Val Fishel. Many thanks also to Ellen's eldest great-granddaughter, Genesis and her husband Amer Hammad for assistance with funding.

Freshwater & Totland Archive Group has sought to identify and acknowledge copyright ownership but this has not always proved possible. Copyright owners are invited to contact the Group so that acknowledgements can be made in any further edition.

c/o Freshwater Library
41 School Green Road
Freshwater
Isle of Wight PO40 9AP
archiverescue@hotmail.co.uk

© Freshwater & Totland Archive Group 2017.

Introduction

The Stevenson family of Hill Lodge, Copse Lane, Freshwater, Isle of Wight

William James Stevenson 1852–1910
Ada Maria Robins Stevenson 1865–1946
Richard Henry Stevenson 1886–
Ada Margaret Stevenson 1891–1971
Ellen Victoria Jane Stevenson 1892–1992
Florence Georgina Geraldine Stevenson 1899–1988
Christopher William Stevenson 1901–

The year 1892 saw Ellen Victoria Jane Stevenson born into a life that was to span one hundred years, a life of twists and turns from its beginning in Portsea and childhood on the Isle of Wight to a peaceful passing in the United States of America. Through Ellen's handwritten journals we are permitted a glimpse into a childhood that would appear to have been idyllic, but secrets revealed later in life show this not necessarily to have been the case.

Ellen's mother, Ada Maria, was herself born in Portsea, in 1865, the youngest of thirteen children born to Jane and Henry Robins. Henry was marine artist to Queen Victoria, and several of his paintings, such as *The Wreck of the Eurydice* and *HMS Victory*, are well known, but what might not be quite so well known is that two of his grandchildren were born in Freshwater.

Married to Irish soldier William Stevenson in Portsea in 1886, Ada Maria Robins, like her mother Jane, experienced thirteen pregnancies but she bore only five children: Richard Henry b. Devonport 1886, Ada Margaret b. Ireland 1891, Ellen Victoria Jane b. Portsea 1892, then Florence Georgina Geraldine b. 1899 and Christopher William b. 1901 both at Hill Lodge, Copse Lane, Freshwater, Isle of Wight.

Ada Maria 1865–1946.

Ada Margaret ('Maggie') 1891–1971.

Ellen Victoria Jane ('Nell') 1892–1992.

Florence Georgina Geraldine
1899–1988.

The Stevenson family lived comfortably at Hill Lodge. While William enjoyed the respect of the men at Fort Victoria and Golden Hill Fort, along with fine furnishings and hunting to hounds, Ada combined managing the home and livestock with concert performances and a social circle that included her good friend a dressmaker of Queen Victoria's court. However, all this came to an end in August 1910 when, the day after admission to Whitecroft asylum, William passed away aged 57 from exhaustion after empyema and pneumonia.

Ada lodging in nearby Priory Road showed commendable concern for her husband, especially considering his fondness for Irish maids and the seduction of her no longer friend the Court dressmaker. However, whether that concern survived the discovery of a pleasure in the company of prostitutes that had considerably depleted her family fortune is uncertain. Nevertheless, while condolences from a couple of these ladies calling at Hill Lodge were politely accepted, their offer of financial assistance was equally politely declined.

The usually sweet-natured Flo had mixed feelings about her father's death. While proud of his military and equine accomplishments she was never to forget how he'd swung her around by her long blonde hair before flinging her across the room, and her references to 'my dear father, may he rot in hell' indicate the hurt felt by his skirt chasing and affairs.

Nell learned of her father's death by her mother silently dropping his maroon uniform sash into her lap. Begging for the sash had become a game between William and Nell when he'd say 'No, no you can't have it yet.' 'When, when can I have it?' she'd ask and the reply was always the same...'When I'm dead.' And so her mother's message was clear. Treasured throughout her lifetime and stained with her tears, the coveted sash is now reduced to little more than a rag and safely in the care of Nell's granddaughter Vicki.

In an attempt to avoid financial ruin, Hill Lodge was adapted to accommodate upper-class guests such as ambassadors, much to the dismay of Flo who, having been accustomed to both an upstairs and a downstairs maid herself, found it degrading to now wait on and clean the shoes of others. However, this indignity was not to last.

As it became clear to Ada that high-class hospitality wasn't going to solve her financial problems, the brave decision was made to give up Hill Lodge and to follow Maggie and Nell, who'd emigrated to the United States of America a year earlier.

Prior to departure aboard RMS *Mauretania* twenty-year-old Maggie appears on the April 1911 census as a servant in the household of Frederick William Robinson of 'Lamorna', Totland Bay, while eighteen-year-old Ellen remains listed at Hill Lodge.

With Ellen's journals written in the latter part of her life, some entries appear to be a little confused, as is often the case with accounts passed down through generations.

Journal One

'I remember Hill Lodge'

Waiting for my father in the Military Service to be placed in a permanent station, we lived in Yarmouth, Isle of Wight, England. Another family, also waiting a transfer, was living there also. They had an older girl than us in their family, and we got to be real friendly. There was three children in our family at the time, the oldest named Richard, next a girl named Ada Margaret and then one named Ellen.

Now, this friend we had met asked Mother's permission to take us to one of the beaches. There were many beaches around this Island where we lived and Mother gave her consent to the nearest one. We were having great fun when she said 'Come, I'll take you to a better place where we can get some baby crabs hiding under big stones.' Well we went and she got a boy she knew there to lift a heavy rock out of the sand – she yelled 'The crabs are in there, reach down and take one home with you.' I put my hand in and they, laughing their heads off, dropped the rock pinning my hand inside.

Yarmouth, Isle of Wight c1900.

Ada – 'Maggie' as she was called then – got very angry and the boy and girl ran away and we were left on the new beach. I could not get loose, nor did we know any way home. Everyone had left and it was getting dark. We were rescued by a beachcomber checking the sands. My entire thumb was open like a book and needed urgent attention.

That was when Mother sat down and told us the facts of life. We were very lucky to have met the man we did instead of some evil person.

Dad got his transfer and we moved to our new home, Hill Lodge, sore thumb and all. Though Mother was fixing our new home, she coddled me a lot for she was sorry she trusted me with that girl.

Hill Lodge – what a place for our adventures.

Here I would explain the exchange of our first names. My mother's name was Ada and my sister Ada Margaret. When he [Dad] would call his wife, sometimes his daughter would go running, so to avoid embarrassment sister Ada was called Margaret, her second name. Of course that ended up being called Maggie and one teacher called her Peggy. So Maggie she became and she did not take her name of Ada till she and I later went to America. My name of Ellen I loved for some reason was changed to Nellie and Nell it has been ever since.

Hill Lodge stood in spacious grounds with a moat two-thirds around it that added to the scenery [and was] lined with fruit trees. All was enclosed with massive white wooden gates and a tall flagpole, flag flying, inside the gate entrance. A wide gravel driveway for carriages led to the front door, with lawns and flower beds in between and [at] the sides of the house.

Barns were there for horses, hay, chickens, turkeys, geese, pigs and cows. There were two kitchens for maids, cooking, laundry etc. All windows were larger than usual and three people could sit in the window seats. Memory of those same windows takes me back to the Boer War. England was having a tough time of it against the Boers because troops had been sent out in such small numbers. Queen Victoria (they said) was crying bitter tears over the loss of men. Finally she gave an order for full attacks ahead, at last success, but a sad one.

Dad and some of the men that had been in India together decided to celebrate on their own and light up Hill Lodge to the skies. He remembered during his rescue of his men in India that one rescued said, as he pointed to a faint light in the sky, 'Better to have one small candle lit than to perish in the dark', so Dad decided to light candles for the men who did not return. Thus the large seats in the windows were used, placing lighted candles along them and the window sills. These candles were twenty inches high from the Army barracks and men were posted to protect against fires, Hill Lodge being quite tall. Outside, men were climbing trees and tying ropes from tree to tree from which they hung many British flags. Crowds gathered and sang hymns till real late. Being young at the time I thought it was a beautiful sight but looking back on it I can see the danger of it. Maybe the yellow ribbons in World War II was better...

Speaking of maids and help Dad had two men for outside work and sometimes paid young servicemen to help who were on furlough, while Mother had two maids and an extra hand when the family got bigger. It was hard to hold a maid for long as we were more in the country, although some we lost from marriage to servicemen; however Dad settled the trouble by hiring Irish girls used to the country life.

Dad would travel to Ireland with Maggie and I and check in with a priest to get good maids hired for Mother, and the maid would travel home with us on the train. A priest would come down to the train for a farewell. Each station after that, a priest would meet the train and talk to us. This went on till we landed home. Next day, after maids would settle in Mother would send them to get acquainted with their own faith in their own church, where they would now attend. So our maids got good protection. They were good help and one we named Lily we grew to love – she was with us for a long time.

This Lily was good in the house and very handy on the land. One day a calf was born and later the mama cow died. The poor little calf would not eat so the maid Lily showed us how to put our hands down in the pail of mash and just leave the tips of our fingers showing and the calf would draw the feed off our fingers. I know Flo and I will not forget that.

Then Dad bought another cow but it would not let the hired help milk it. So Lily again came to the rescue and sang to it while she milked it and the cow chewed and mooed and let the milk down... Lily milked the cow and got extra pay, the hired hand named 'Twaddle' was given more yard work.

There was no central heating in those days but large open fireplaces in each room, also in maids' rooms. Coal used for heating was kept [in a barn] called the bins. It was filled with tons of coal and wood the year around. All cooking and laundry was done on iron coal stoves. This coal was delivered in large lump squares, not small as it is today. A block would be put on a lit fire and when it heated through could be tapped by a poker and broken into pieces thus giving us a roaring fire to enjoy.

The fireplaces were white and grey marble. Birds were fastened on each side with brass studs. These birds were the size of pigeons and Mother would remove them from time to time to have them cleaned.

Across the mantle border was a macramé strip also fastened to it with brass studs. Holes had been drilled into the marble for that purpose. The birds looked as [though] they were flying. The macramé was made, and given to Mother, by servicemen who brought it all from India.

Rooms were furnished with mahogany furniture and the lighting was furnished by oil lamps – no electricity on the island at that time. These lamps were hung up in center of rooms, with cords and pulleys attached. Cords led from lamps across the ceiling and down sides of walls in a corner with pulley attached. Lamps could be raised or lowered and held in that position by the pulleys. Quite an idea, believe me!

All water was obtained from several pumps in the wells and piped through pipes for house toilets. All other water for use was drawn right from the pumps.

One of the rooms toward the rear of the house was transferred into a playroom for children so noise would be at a minimum in front of house. By this time Mother had two more children, a dear little sister named Florence, who we call Flo, though Mother soon gave her the name of 'Little Peace Maker', a name to be found true as time passed on; then a little son, Christopher.

Our playroom was divided into spaces. It reached all along the side of the house at the back with plenty of space. One wall was a shelf for toys for the boys, when not in use, another for girls on second wall. Real end of room was for larger toys.

At the other end Dad had installed an American coal stove to heat the room instead of an open fireplace (it would be safer). We had plenty of room in the center and sometimes Mother would put a round table in the middle and give a party for our dolls.

This 'Hill Lodge' had been built for members of the Royal Family, later being used by Lords and Ladies and military men in high positions. They sure allowed room for everything, wanting things bigger and better than anyone else. Walls so thick no heavy firing of military guns could bother them although it was surrounded by Golden Hill Fort and Yarmouth's Fort Victoria.

Golden Hill Fort interior c1925. E A Sweetman

One feature of the dining room I'll mention. The fireplace stood central at the back wall. One side of it was a waiter's cupboard, half of it opening into a shelf the size of a small table, and another door on the other end Mother could not get open.

The first door with shelf was fine. It was a pass into the kitchen where maids could put hot food on [the] shelf, come to [the] dining area and serve, not having to go and come through a long corridor. The other turned out to be a secret door leading to the upstairs rooms.

Brother Richard found it out first. He was playing near the fireplace, when putting his hand on the wall to get up, he by chance pressed a secret button. He fell into the wall and the door closed on him. After a long search for him around the grounds one searcher told Mother he heard crying in the walls but very faint, then Richard was rescued and told what happened.

Neither Dad nor Mother knew of this secret, so Mother had the place closed off and a small cupboard built in front where she kept cases of several kinds of cookies and liquor. This she guarded with a key.

So much for the mystery house – ha, ha!

Leaving the dining room we enter a den on the left, then a long corridor with rooms off it. One held only hooks for meat such as from pigs, turkeys and chickens raised on the place; another long, cold grey slates that held pans of milk, same for half and one pound pats of butter. Next, rows on rows of hooks to hold rows of onions shipped to Hill Lodge from France to last a year and braided together.

Back of [the] corridor near first kitchen [were] rooms for lamp cleaning, shoe polishing [and] repair work, and toilets for the women. Wash basins and jugs were provided for women on a stand in their room, for cleansing, and a tub for baths.

Toilets for men were in an outside building and as they lived in the village there was no need to have them enter the home.

Bathrooms in those days were unknown. We just had toilet, and wash bowls upstairs. Large metal tubs were hung on the walls of a corridor side downstairs. They would be taken upstairs [and] placed on heavy mats. Then hot and cold water pails got carried up for baths and of course had to be disposed of again.

When my sister Flo and brother Chris were born, Dad took two rooms from the corridor (originally beer and cider rooms) and had a bathroom built. [He] ordered a bath tub seven feet long from Portsmouth, all white [with] brass fittings, and hired men to install it.

This was supposed to be a birthday gift for Mother but who got the luxury of the first bath – why Dad! Of course! As this was the beginning of stationary bath tubs for England, Mother was pestered a lot by friends wanting to see it. Some never heard of it.

I have already mentioned the moat that was around the house, well that moat has a special memory. A large lot of green grass was beside it and Dad had it kept cut like a lawn so we could play there. Plum trees full of fruit were growing along the edge. Such large plums, we heard later those trees came from Italy. Some we used to knock off with sticks to eat and some of course fell into the moat.

One day my brother fixed up a net and was planning to reach the larger ones by standing on a horse. Maggie, Ada, wanted the field cleared so she could do some horse tricks. Richard went up to her and blew a horn in her horse's ear. The next thing Maggie had been thrown into the moat of murky running water and had to be rescued fast. When Dad arrived, she was yelling 'I broke my arm and my shoulder is broken.' Dad took her to the house and sent his man for the doctor.

After a good examination she had only got wet and a bruise on her arm. The deep water had saved her from injury. The doctor said 'Now Maggie, there is one more test I must make', and Maggie asked 'Will you put a lot of bandages on me please, like you did for Nellie's eye?' Doctor said 'I'll do what is necessary. Tell me, how far can you lift that arm without pain?' Maggie raised her arm a little and said 'Right there.' When doctor asked 'How far before you fell?' Maggie tossing her arm up high said 'Way up there.' Doctor said 'Fine, come to me and I will start the treatment.' He took Maggie across his lap upside down and spanked her good. Picking up his satchel, he said 'There will be no charge', and he left. Maggie said 'I don't care, Nellie gets doctors often and this time he came to see me!' Years later and I could not figure that one out. If only she knew how I envied her good health.

School was a mile and a half walk from Hill Lodge in one direction and church was a mile in the other. Sunday was a busy walking day for us. Dad would walk us to service in the morning and back for noon. Then children would go to Sunday school in the afternoon where we watched babies being baptised and heard the wedding banns said for coming weddings. Home for tea and then Mother went with us to the evening service.

Then on Wednesdays we went to St Andrew's military church with all military men and Dad in full uniform, watching them form fours on church grounds and parade before they marched back to their barracks.

Also we loved to go with Dad to Fort Victoria and watch the men drill and be put through their manoeuvers. Men in this fort were all

All Saints' Parish Church, Freshwater c1900.

Catholic and Dad in charge was a Protestant. These men all loved Dad and respected him, so there was no religious fuss.

However, Maggie once again upset the apple cart. She rode a horse right into the barrack square with yellow ribbons in her hair and yellow ribbons decked out all over the horse as she said it was Orangeman's Day and she wanted to celebrate it as yellow orange was the emblem of the Protestant.

Dad said he was 'sweating blood' as to the outcome of this! However, every man rose and stood at attention in front of her, saluted her, and then turned and saluted Dad. Believe me, there was tears in his eyes as he took the reins and slowly led her out of the compound.

Maggie, Ada, was a great horse lover and while Mother was planning a few house chores for us to do Maggie would be gone down to the barn polishing brass work on the harnesses in an old dress, her lovely blonde hair down her back tied with a string, and singing her heart out.

Dad had bought a racehorse to ride to the fox hunts. This racer had been abused while the owner was in Europe and became nervous, which is bad for a racer, so the owner sold it to Dad. In no time Maggie had it OK again.

At first she was the only one who could get near it but handled it so gently that no matter where he was she would call him and he would come running to her and put his nose in her neck. That was more than Dad could do for a long time.

Riding for miles with no saddle and times no bridle, [she] guided [him] by her voice and a pat on the neck and her hanging on to his mane; friends used to say 'Maggie, you're an Indian.'

Around this time, my brother Richard was training a horse up in the top training field, had it tied to a post with long rope for jumping. I entered the field on the wrong side just as Richard tapped the horse to move it and it, getting scared, ran around me wrapping the ropes around my knees. Richard tried to turn him the other way. My yells did not help any; the horse broke loose and galloped down the paddock dragging me along.

St Andrew's Garrison Church, Freshwater c1950. © G Foskett

Fort Victoria, Freshwater c1905. F N Broderick

In its panic it dashed through a thick hedge and on to the main road with me still in the looped rope. Some soldiers saw me, rushed the horse and, though they were knocked down, managed to stop it. They brought me home on somebody's back door, called the military doctor and I was in doctors' [care] and on crutches for six months. It was entirely my own fault knowing I should not enter when training was on.

Dear little Flo, what a great help to me. Putting her dolls away she gave a lot of attention to me. Sitting beside me she would read her picture books to me and give me all the details of the new baby chicks just hatched. Once in a while she would give me one to hold and then get one for herself. I often wonder, with all the hugs and squeezes we gave those chicks, if they ever grew up to be hens.

My Godmother, knowing about the chicks, brought Flo and I a couple of pigeons of our own. Flo and I would wrap their wings down with a cloth and then dress them in bonnets and cloaks like dolls, and Flo would wheel them in her dolls carriage.

When I finally got better Flo and I would get to the beach and have great times together. I would sit in a chair and Flo would build me a sandcastle. She would paddle a bit in the water, later tossing her hair ribbon in the sea and calling it her boat. Later, waves beating in would wash her castle away and we would scramble to get out of there. Much later in years I was writing a book of poems and remembering that face that day, I wrote a poem on it. May I enter it now?

'Be polite to me', says Flo

A little girl played by the side of the sea
Making sand cakes for afternoon tea
A wooden spoon in her hand
And a little pail to hold the sand.

She seemed all alone, in this world of sand
Other kiddies around her would stand
To watch the castle she fashioned there
While the warm wind blew through her hair.

Blonde hair, brown eyes, a face so sweet
Sun-tanned arms and legs and feet
With giggles of laughter and shouts of glee
Hair ribbons she used as boats in the sea.

In came the tide with a mighty roar
Up to her castle and through the door
While the little girl ran with all her might
Saying 'Mr Sea that was not right
If next time on the sand I'll be,
You better be more polite to me.'

Ellen Victoria Jane Stevenson

The Little Lady of Hill Lodge

My Flo she stands upon the stair
With tender delight in her eyes
The donkey and cart are waiting outside
To take her on one of her country rides.

She stands on that stair with an air of grace
With a pretty white veil framing her face
Her sweet little smile is precious to see
And I am proud to know she belongs to me.

There is no-one I know that could compare
With that 'Little Lady' that stood on the stair.

My dear little sister Flo.

Ellen Victoria Jane Stevenson

Flo and the donkey cart

Dad bought Flo a donkey and cart of her own and she soon learned how to manage it. The donkey's coat was kept clipped short and groomed like a horse and the cart was shaped round and six could sit in it. Flo taught that donkey so it knew every word and move from Flo. Sometimes Dad would take Flo in the cart to the country club to bring home ledgers. Dad was president of the club.

Flo would say 'Dad, don't stay too long in there. My donkey won't wait for you.' Well, Dad would promise and then forget and Flo, getting tired, would cluck the reins and say 'Let's go home, Jinny', and then Flo would snuggle down and Jinny would take off and land up safe at Hill Lodge with Flo fast asleep. Her Dad had to walk home carrying the ledgers.

Once, while out together, Dad met a friend, a Lord and Lady Hamilton, and stopped to chat for a while. Then trying to draw their attention to his daughter, he said 'Come, Florence, where are your manners? Won't you say goodbye to my friends?' Flo, who wore a little white veil over her face, lifted her veil and said, 'How can I, Papa? I do not know them and have not been introduced to them.' 'Well put,' said Lady Hamilton and they walked on. Dad was furious but Mama pointed out the bad manners was from Dad. His daughter should have been introduced at the beginning. She then asked that introductions should be used to all of us at any time as she had forbidden us to talk to strangers.

After Flo had used her donkey and cart for three years, Mother was telling us of a little boy that had fell off a cliff and injured his back and could not sit up or walk. I thought at first it was a warning for us to stay clear of the cliffs but Flo surprised us.

After sitting quiet for a while she said 'Mother, give Jinny and my cart to that little boy. If his daddy would put boards across the seats, he could lie down and Jinny could take him for rides.' Well after waiting a few days to see if she was still willing, Mother and Flo drove down and gave her Jinny and cart to the little boy. That's my Flo and she has been that way all her life.

Mother's pear tree

Looking out our playroom window, we could see a pear tree loaded with fruit. This of all the fruit trees was special, planted for Mother at the corner of the house, and the fruit had a great taste. Also, Mother had planted a bed of bluebells under it. Richard, Maggie and I were told 'not to touch that tree'. Although we had all different fruits we could eat, one could see we coveted that one. So – Richard and I had a plan – he would take a hoe and climb out of the playroom window on the second floor on his stomach, and I would hold onto his legs to balance him and he would get us some pears. Well, we were all set when Dad walked in, pushed me on one side and took hold of Richard but Richard, trying to get away, fell out of the window and dragged Dad with him. Just then Mother drove up and said Dad was 'as bad as his son'. Neither Dad nor Richard told on me. Thank goodness...

***

My mother was a concert singer, taking male and female parts in a song. One part very high singing and the next deep down in her chest. Sometimes Dad would like to have people passing by the house believe he was singing with her, but they soon found out when they went to her concerts.

She wore lovely evening dresses and velvet cloaks – had them in different colours – and Flo and I would ask her to be a dolly for us when she came home. She surprised us one Christmas by giving us dolls dressed just like her and the same colours. Speaking of dolls reminds me, 'the military' used to give a Christmas party for us every year. Many children, with parents, were there. They used to call us kids 'the Army Brats'. They got the largest tree they could find – the Island was loaded with them – and set it up in one of the barracks. They would provide tea, milk, cake and cookies and each child, when leaving for home, was given a stocking with orange, nuts and candy. The big attraction of course was the presents on the tree. There was always a special doll on the tree for Flo and I, and a book or skipping rope for Maggie, who did not like dolls. It was a long time before we found out that the presents were donated by the children's parents. Before we went home we danced and sang some songs and Mother played the piano for us. The piano was loaned by a merchant and we had a grand time.

Mother, seeing how we liked dancing around, decided she would give us dancing lessons, which were held in our drawing room. Dad came home in the middle of it and said 'No dancing. Let these children study. This carpet is not for scuffling.' The carpet was an oriental one – brought from Europe. Then he said 'Get to bed.'

Mother was so annoyed she had the carpet picked up the next day and a regular carpet [put] in its place. Next dance time Dad came in and before he could say a word Mother said 'This is our home, my piano, my carpet, and our children are enjoying themselves.' Dad left, and days later he asked if he could join us and teach us 'ballroom dancing'. Having made this sort of apology, we all had a good time.

Sometimes when Mother would be singing at one of her concerts and the maids were in their quarters, Richard and I would sneak downstairs, take the top off a loaf of fresh bread, take a jar of jam and pilfer some thick cream in a bowl. Then back to the toy room and have a feast. New bread, jam and cream on top – yummy! We never included Maggie, so when she found out she told Mother – and she caught us red-handed the next night. We were so scared we dropped everything in a mess down the front stairs, on maroon velvet carpet. This on top of the pear tree episode was a little too much for Mother and she grounded us from all fun – sports, plays and parties – for a whole week.

***

I would like to tell of the royal Romany gypsies that travelled to England to visit with British Royalty. It was a Prince and Princess and their attendants. They preferred to live gypsy style instead of hotels – bringing their own style with them, wanted to be in open pastures. So an arrangement was made for the caravans etc to be brought into our upper pasture land and they camped out there for days between visits to London.

They were very interesting people, wore beautiful clothes and good jewellery. They talked quite a little to Mother of their travels, and their attendants would put on a play for us children, singing songs. I used to plague them by running up and down the steps of their caravan, while Flo would play with some of the beads they gave her.

Freshwater School

Our school, as I have already mentioned, was a one and a half mile walk from Hill Lodge, so we carried a lunch and sometimes bought a lunch prepared by pupils in a cooking lesson. We had many classes in that school planned for different days: prayers, religion, arithmetic, essay writing, spelling, poetry, reading, sewing, cooking, history, geography and field trips for birds, plants and leaves, dumbbell exercising and swimming. Games in recess were run by teachers.

All Saints' School, Freshwater c1900.

We were marched in twos down to the beach a mile from the school on Wednesday and taught in the ocean to swim by instructors. We had little huts in which to change into swimsuits.

These houses were little huts on wheels and when not in use was kept up on a walkway. They had pulleys and ropes attached to them and when needed was wheeled down and into entrance of sea. There was a door to enter from the sand and another door opposite to step into the ocean. There was hooks inside to hang up clothes and two long benches on sides for seats. One hut could accommodate four persons at a time.

Material for sewing, knitting etc was all found by the school. Parents were asked if they cared to buy any finished garment we would make, for only the price of the material – much less than if bought in a store. If so, that money would be put back into the school. If not, a yearly sale would be held and proceeds put back on the ledger.

Colwell Bay, Freshwater c1900.

I learned to knit when I was four years old and made many useful things while at school. Our sewing classes included patterns, which we made with newspapers on each other and then cut our garments from these patterns. In those days many folks made their own patterns as they were rare and expensive. These home patterns worked well and were a very good fit.

The cooking classes were held for the older grades starting with vegetables, soups, meats, fish, cookies, bread, and buns – later on butterscotch candy. This cooking was for teachers' free lunch but any students who wished could enjoy a meal for a penny.

Our grades were different from America. We had standards for our classes. By Standard 7, one should be old enough and well taught to leave school with a fair education. I was not old enough to leave when I reached Standard 7 so I taught there in Standard 3 for one and a half years, and was teaching my young brother Chris when I realised my class was in awe of me. Meaning to find the reason was simple. Chris had told them 'That's my sister. You better watch out in her class. She can be real mean if you don't.' So much for brotherly love...

Maggie at the time often laughed and talked about two red hats mother had bought us. They were the same and we had hoped to wear them the following Sunday, but Sunday Mom said 'No, it looks like rain. Wear your blue ones.' Well Dad took Mom riding to a neighbour and I went to service in my blue hat. Maggie showed up later with her red hat.

My, how the rain did pour on our way home... With her red hat flopping about her ears, she ran into the house and came out with a second red hat on her head. Her hair and face was all dye from the first wet hat, so I knew she was wearing my new hat. I accused her of taking mine and the fight began.

These hats had elastic bands that went under the chin and Mom used to mark mine on the inside, also my clothes, because being one year apart we were much the same size. Knowing this, I took hold of the elastic and tried to pull it off her head. She backed away screaming and holding on for dear life and I would not release the elastic.

Right then Mother and Dad entered the front drive. I told Dad why I was pulling like that. Dad raised his whip and said 'Miss, let go this instant.' Well, I did and poor Maggie got it right in her neck. Dad took the hat, and her red-dyed hair came tumbling down.

Whenever we fought, Mother would sit us down and order a 'debate'. Maggie's hat was found. She was guilty as charged but forgiven because I had punished her and was guilty of hurting her. So case was closed right there and we kissed and made up.

***

Now came the time when Richard, Maggie and I were entered into St Joseph's College at Totland.

Professor Buisseret took away our first names, only using surnames and giving us numbers for our first. So Richard the eldest became Stevenson No. 1, Maggie was No. 2 and I was No. 3. When any member gave trouble their surname and number was placed on a blackboard for demerits. If 'Stevenson' appeared on the board, all three of us would hold our breath till the number would be added on.

Then the one in trouble could take a caning or pay a fine. Fines would be placed in a locked box. If unable to pay right away, one was allowed to sign an IOU to be paid in two weeks. So we were careful not to cut down too much on our allowance. Maggie, however, was always teasing the son of the Professor and putting IOUs in the penalty box. It got so high Dad took away her allowance and that meant several canings for her. Later the Professor told Dad 'My, what a change in Maggie. She is behaving so well she must be sick.'

We would play games of ground hockey and tennis. The school divided into two teams and the winning side would receive the contents of the penalty box as a reward. My, could that Maggie play hockey and tennis.

St Joseph's School, Amos Hill, Totland Bay c1915.

Like all good things, they sometimes have to come to an end. After a long illness from an accident we lost our Dad.

We gave up Hill Lodge and Maggie and I left for America and was followed the next year by Mother, Flo and Christopher... all planning now to lead a different life but where, if kept together, it might turn out to be still a happy one.

I heard later that Hill Lodge was used as a hospital during the war by officers. Later it was taken over by a firm raising small horses to be sold in Europe.

The name of 'Hill Lodge' was on British [maps] but now being commercial they have been told to call it Hill Farms as it is no longer royal. So now 'Hill Farms' is on British maps of the Isle of Wight.

I have seen later photos of Hill Lodge since leaving it and much of its beauty has been discarded.

The great driveway for carriages, and center gardens of flowers, has been neglected and looks sort of lonely now.

The bluebells under Mom's favourite pear tree were something to see and should a traveller go visiting South England don't miss seeing the violets that grow there wild with their beautiful perfume. Also primroses in different colours, and cowslips. I think they help to make England. It did for me.

Oh yes, my dears, I remember Hill Lodge...

Finis

Journal Two

Ellen's second account, written in Ohio at age 92 and typed by daughter-in-law Elinor Bruggeman, duplicates some earlier entries.

My dad's parents were Richard Stevenson and Anna Whiteside of Scotland, who inherited a farm in Ireland and their children were born in Lurgan, County Armagh, Ireland. They had four sons and three daughters:

William – my dad who was in Army.

Edward – Irish Chief of Police in Dublin.

Christopher – on the farm.

David – sheep owner in Canada (brother Dave's daughter married Lloyd George Prime Minister of England).

Anne – nurse to Vanderbilt's in America.

Ellen – also with the Vanderbilt's and returned to marry a farm owner.

Margaret – married to Lord Ford and now has title of 'Lady Margaret'.

My dad was born in 1852 and left home when he was 13 years old to join the Army. He was sent with the 18th Royal Irish Regiment to India and served there for 21 years. He became an officer before he returned home, was in many wars and got many medals and citations, although he often said he was 'not sure if he deserved the Good Conduct medal'. He was also through the Egyptian Gordon Relief campaigns and the Afghan. He received medals and a star for them also, including the long service one.

On one upset a call came to say that some of his men had been ambushed in a culvert and faced certain death – this was the Battle of the Nile.[1] He called for volunteers to join him in a small ship carrying supplies to rescue them.

[1] *For 'Battle of the Nile' read Nile Expedition 1884–1885.*

Silver Replica. © V Knopf

To his surprise the whole troop stepped forward saying they would follow him.

Only a few could be selected. A priest standing near said, 'Stevenson, we are different faiths but you know I am praying to the same God for your success.' Dad answered 'Thank you, Father, but I have not done as good as I could and maybe the prayers might fall off me like water off a duck's back.' However, the Father started praying just the same. This was told us later by one of his men.

The Nile was real deep with water [some places] and other places not so bad so that at times the men swam and pushed the vessel ahead of them and at other places carried it on their shoulders like a casket.

The mission was a great success and the men were saved. Later on returning to England, Dad and the men were given a great ovation.

The government had a replica of that ship cast in silver and presented to Dad for his men in their name.

Dad asked that the silver replica be held at headquarters for future troops to see and asked that a framed, large photograph be given each man including himself with an inscription on it to hold as their own. This was done and my father's copy is now hanging on the wall in his grandson Louis Bruggeman's house in Medina, Ohio, USA.

After 21 years in India he returned to England and continued his military life, later being made Chief Barrack Warden of the Western Forts in England including Fort Victoria and Golden Hill Fort in the Isle of Wight.

In 1886 he married Ada Robins, who was a noted concert singer and sang for both male and female parts in opera: very high for the lady and low and deep for the male parts in the same songs. This couple became my parents.

Her dad, my grandfather, was marine artist to Queen Victoria, who commissioned him to paint pictures of old-time ships which she had hung in Windsor Castle. Later he did the same for heads of other countries as well.

Mom's mother, my grandmother, was Lady Jane Proux of Cherbourg, France. Grandpa was titled 'Sir' and Grandma was still titled 'Lady', this time in England, and could be passed on to future females in her line, passing from one to the other. The family crest was the Mailed Fist that could be used on carriages, stationery, silverware, or door entrances. Also the three feather insignia that has become the crest of all Princes of Wales. Dad and Mom never used these crests, although my mother was entitled to do so.

When Mother would be singing in the house Dad would try to make passers-by think it was him, but they soon found him out when they went to Mom's concerts.

Dad was a great horseman. He loved to race and go for hunting. We lived on a large estate and there were acres of land for him to devote his time to, and the horses. This place was called Hill Lodge, previously owned by royal families, and is entered on the map of the

Isle of Wight, South of England. Cows, pigs, ducks and turkeys were kept for our use. Brave a soldier as Dad became, you should have seen him disappear when Mom asked him to kill a chicken.

I'll never forget the time of the Boer War. England was having a tough time against the Boers because the British troops were being sent out in small garrisons. Queen Victoria was crying bitter tears on the outcome. Finally she took charge and gave an order of full steam ahead.

Finally a victory, and then Dad and some of the men he had in India and several new soldiers broke out in a ceremony of their own.

During the rescue of his men in India, he remembered a small light up in the sky and one of the rescued said 'It was a blessing, like a little candle. Better to have one candle lit than to perish in the dark.' Remembering this, Dad and his men decided to light the skies with burning candles in honour of those who did not return.

Hill Lodge had fifteen large rooms with very large window sills. The men got long, thick candles and placed rows of them on all the sills and lit them all, having men in each room to prevent fires. Outside men were climbing trees and tying ropes from one to the other on which they hung British flags and crowds gathered and sang hymns till real late.

Being young at the time I thought it was a beautiful sight, but looking back I can see the danger of it. Maybe the yellow ribbons of World War ll was better.

My dad was injured, broken ribs from a falling horse, but would not admit it. He took his troops the next day on an inspection of the first planes in England and got caught in a very bad storm. Instead of getting aid to come home he stayed at a barracks and over a roaring open fire he stood until his uniform was dry. Later he came down with pneumonia. Regimental doctors gave their services, removed ribs, but were unable to save him.

After 46 years of military service he passed away and was buried with high military honours in the Parkhurst Military Cemetery, August 11th 1910.

This August 11th has a great part in my memories:

Grandpa Stevenson died August 11th 1892 in the morning.

Grandpa Robins died August 11th 1892 in the evening.

My son Louis Bruggeman born August 11th 1924.

My mother passed away August 11th 1946.

Death notice of William Stevenson

'The death occurred at Carisbrooke on Friday last after a long illness of Barrack Warden William Stevenson who was known and greatly respected here by both soldiers and civilians. The late Mr Stevenson had been Chief Barrack Warden at Fort Victoria, Isle of Wight, for the past 16 years and until recently resided at Hill Lodge, Norton. A little over a month ago he went to Bournemouth with his fellow officers and caught a severe cold on top of a rib accident which developed into pneumonia from which he died. Stevenson was formerly in the 18th Royal Irish Regiment. He was through the Afghan and Egyptian Gordon Relief campaigns and received medals and star for them, also the good conduct and long service medal. The deceased was a staunch Conservative and for several years was treasurer of the Conservative Club in Freshwater, Isle of Wight. His loss will be widely mourned. A deep sympathy is felt for his wife and five children. His age was 59 years.[2]

The funeral took place with high military honours at the Military Cemetery in Park[hurst]. Many friends were present among them Captain Maloney ASC,[3] Lieutenant Bissett with a corps of NC Officers, men from the 22nd Company of [Fort] Victoria and officers and men from the 22nd Suffolk Regiment, and the Barrack Wardens of the Island acted as bearers. Many wreaths from friends — Mr & Mrs Tanner, RE Officers, Sergeant of Royal Engineers Fort Victoria, Sergeants Mess of Golden Hill, all sent flowers. Messrs H & P Damp, of Newport, carried out the funeral arrangements.'

[2] *William Stevenson died age 57.*

[3] *Army Service Corps.*

Mother a widow

After Dad passed away the government took my younger brother, Christy, into Military School. Mother decided the extensive parties etc of the past would be stopped. So-called friends then deserted Mother and turned to others. As I was educated in St Joseph's College, I decided to look for a position to help me later on. Folks would not take me serious and did not think it was necessary. So Ada and I decided to try out in the North of England. I wrote to my Aunt Anne in America to tell her what I wished to do and what she thought of the idea. She replied with a large amount of money and the request that I come to America. Later on I received a letter from Aunt Nell, also in America, saying that she was upset that she was not given the opportunity to help me, but if sister Ada would accompany me she would cover her expenses. So we packed for our trip. Mother and sister moved into a smaller house we had in Totland. Christy was in Military School, my older brother Richard was in India in Military Service, so we were all separated.

On our way to America our ship the *Mauretania* was hit by tidal waves that did a lot of damage. We were all ordered to get down below of the decks and the sides were bound with ropes to hold us safe. One man who refused the Captain's orders was taken in by force and later to be found with broken arms. At least his life was saved. When we again were allowed to come on deck we saw everything... we saw rugs, chairs and folks' belongings way out on the ocean like little boats. Great damage was done to the ship itself and the huge rails were bent and twisted beyond repair. The trip took five and a half days and we sure were happy when we were able to land.

Ada and Nell in America

Being separated from Mother and Flo got hard for us to take so a year later Mother took our brother Christy out of Military School and with Flo all three joined us in the States and we set up housekeeping in Manchester, Connecticut.

Ada and I were employed in Cheney Velvet Mill. Ada was a velvet inspector and shipper while I ran a typewriter and comptometer in the office.

Sister Flo took after Mother in the music line and often accompanied Mother in concerts. She made music her life work playing piano and Wurlitzer organ in theaters. Many times she became the support of the family. She married and continued her theater work while Mother ran the house and cared for Flo's two children.

Mother passed away in 1946 and then Flo and I and children moved to California, each having our own homes. Living alone I had a bad accident, disposed of my home and lived with my Flo who cared for me for 12 years. Then Flo had almost the same accident. Her daughter is with her now and I was sent to live with my son and wife in Ohio. A great difference in the weather, but happy to be here with Elinor and Louis. At 92 years things are easier for me so I am using my time to record anecdotes to pass on to the children.

Cheney Velvet Mill.

Mother cancelled booking on *Titanic*

When my mother decided to join us in America she booked passage on the *Titanic*. After she had all packed and ready she had what she called one of her 'dreams'. Her body turned cold and she saw the *Titanic* with folks on board and having a merry time. Suddenly there was a vast shape in the water and the *Titanic* was ruined. All started to panic and she saw their frightened faces.

She heard bugles blowing and the hymn 'Nearer my God to Thee' drifting toward her. Rousing, she told Flo she was cancelling their trip on the *Titanic*. This she did and stayed with a friend till she could book her trip on the *New York*.

Expecting them to come, we were lost at the news of the *Titanic* and wanted to go from Connecticut to New York to see if we could get news of them. Our factory owner told us 'No! Stay where you are. Better chance of getting news that way.' Many of our fellow workers

Poster advertising the *Olympic* and the *Titanic*, 1912.

Canvas bag worn by Ada beneath her skirts to carry precious documents on the voyage. © B Huntsinger

stood out in our street with lighted lanterns to keep us company. Later a cablegram arrived at the factory saying our family was not on the *Titanic*, although the ship's records had Mrs Stevenson and children on their list. A week after that they arrived and the town turned their folks out to meet them.[4]

Mother often had what she called 'dreams' and saved us many mishaps and heartaches by these forewarnings.

Our family kept very close together losing sister Ada 1971 and Mother 1946.

My brother Richard

My brother Richard was the eldest of many children, but only five of us lived. Like her mother before her, mine had thirteen births. My brother Christopher was the youngest [and] now lives in Canada. Richard was a premature birth due to an accident and my parents had quite a time raising him. It seems that Dad was going in full dress uniform down the stairs and Mother being pregnant was teasing him to kiss her goodbye when she reached out for him, overbalanced, and fell on his sword on her stomach as they rolled down the stairs together. They rushed to the Military Hospital and Richard was born but carried around for weeks on a pillow, and no one but nursing staff was allowed to touch him. He was named Richard Henry after my father's dad. He turned out real well in schooling [and] attended St Joseph's College with me. Later he was sent to Scotland to further his education and won the College of Preceptors – a great honor.

Then, like many of our men ahead of him, he joined the Royal Garrison Artillery.

Dad, who had quite a career behind himself as well, went to London to petition for his son to be taken into his old regiment which with Richard's education would entitle him to Officer ranks but my brother, who had an altercation over my sister with his dad, refused, saying he would stay with the RGA and make his career on his own.

---

[4] *Ada, Florence and Christopher Stevenson departed Southampton bound for New York aboard SS New York on 11th May 1912.*

Badge of the Royal Garrison Artillery.

So as a private soldier he was sent to India and spent many years there away from us.

Many letters came home describing the life there and the wars that would come up.

General Allenby, hearing of his education, took him to be his private secretary, which made my brother very happy. He then travelled everywhere with the General. He was with General Allenby when the General and his forces walked through the gates of Jaffa after he had defeated the Turks and their Teuton allies.[5]

My brother said the General had all his men dismount and walk as he did himself, and accepting the enemy's surrender also refrained from taking the sword of the defeated tendered to him telling my brother it was not necessary from a good warrior, that the surrender was indeed enough. Richard wrote later – 'it was indeed a great

[5] *Fall of Jerusalem December 1917.*

pleasure and privilege to serve under so honourable a man as General Allenby'. Later, in another campaign, my brother's letters stopped.

A friend of my mother suggested she write to the War Office for news of her son, which we did and was told General Allenby and troops were lost in battle, that Richard's name and number 23058 would be held as missing in action. Should different news arrive they would notify her.

Citations and medals were being held for the men and after some years passed would be sent to her – unless of course he had married and then they would be sent to his widow and any children he might have had.

Years went along and still no word.

Finally I decided to get some kind of an answer but Mother asked me not to do so. All the time she had no word she had faith that he was alive, but news that he had passed on was more than she could take. So, giving my word on this we are still at a loss.

What happened to Richard?

Henry Robins

Ex Provost Sergt. Henry Robins, Royal Marine Artillery.

First man to enlist in the British Service in the reign of Her Majesty Queen Victoria, 4.45 am 20th June 1837; discharged 10th February 1860, anniversary of Her Majesty's wedding day. The first inventor of the Mittrailleuse Gatling & Nordenfeldt Guns – see "United Service Gazette" 1861, 1870 and "Hampshire Telegraph" 1880. From photo taken 1848. Marine Artist to Her Most Gracious Majesty the Queen and H.R.H the Prince of Wales.

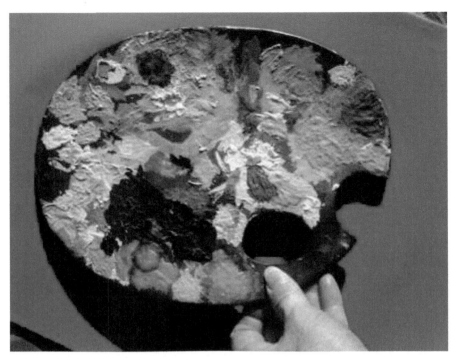

Henry Robins' palette, passed down through his family. © B Huntsinger

My mother's dad, my grandfather, was born in Chichester, England in 1820. He left home on 20th June 1837 to join the Royal Marine Artillery. The first man to enlist on the day of Her Majesty's accession to the throne, Queen Victoria, Mr Robins served his Queen and country for 23 years in military and naval service. During that time he took part in seventeen general engagements and obtained many citations and medals, including good conduct and China medals for the Boxer Rebellion.[6] He left the service on 10th February 1860, the anniversary of Queen Victoria's wedding.

Henry Robins had become quite an artist in painting. Being both marine and naval he met and became good friends with Prince Edward — son of Queen Victoria. After long talks together the Prince

[6] For 'Boxer Rebellion' read Opium War 1839–42.

Osborne
August 16 1878

Lt. General Ponsonby is
commanded by The
Queen to state that
Her Majesty is much
pleased with the
sketch of the naval
review Executed by
Mr Robins.

Letter from Lt. Gen. Henry Ponsonby, Queen Victoria's Private Secretary, to Henry Robins 16th August 1878. © B Huntsinger

45

said, 'Robins you are great fun, how would you like to meet your Queen?' Grandpa answered 'That is my dearest wish, but a good one. I hope I will never be without her likeness in my pocket.'

So a promise was given and kept and a meeting with the Queen was arranged.

After a few meetings and talks she became very interested in his art and commissioned him to paint pieces of old-time ships and sea pieces for her, which she hung in Windsor Castle.

He then did paintings for other heads of other countries, as well as the Prince of Wales. Letters and telegrams he received from her and others are now being held by my sister Flo in California.

Many of his paintings were of ships on which he gave service while in the marines.

He was present in the fight of Spring and Langan[7] and at the launching of HMS *Charlotte*,[8] volunteered to colonise Port Essington in Australia[9] and [was] a volunteer for the Chinese war.[10] [He] bought his discharge from the Army and entered the Metropolitan Police Force, which he later resigned and rejoined the Marines.

After he embarked on the ship *Styx* and served two years on the coast of West Africa, he returned to England, married and was sent to Chatham, England.

Six months later [he] was returned to Portsmouth Headquarters and was made one of the Honor Guards of the opening of the New Steam Basin.[11] He was in charge of calls at Grunswarf Barracks[12] and made one of the Guards of Honor at the Duke of Wellington's

---

[7] *Tom Spring and John Langan 'threw their hat into the ring' to fight over seventy bareknuckle rounds in 1824, first in Worcester then again in Chichester, with Tom Spring the victor on both occasions.*

[8] *HMS Princess Charlotte launched September 1825.*

[9] *Port Essington colonised 1837.*

[10] *Chinese war 1839–1842.*

[11] *New Steam Basin opened 1848.*

[12] *Gunwharf Barracks.*

Present Address:

H. ROBINS,

MARINE ARTIST TO HER MAJESTY THE QUEEN

AND

H.R.H. THE PRINCE OF WALES

LATE

396, COMMERCIAL ROAD, LANDPORT.

Patronized by their Majesties the King and Queen of Denmark, their Serene Highnesses the Prince and Princess Edward of Saxe-Weimar, Rear-Admiral the Hon. F. A. Foley, Admiral Montagu O'Reilly, Lieut.-General G. A. Schomberg, C.B., General Sir G. Willis, Lord C. Beresford, Colonel Wood, C.B., 10th Royal Hussars, Admiral J. O. Hopkins, Admiral G. O. Wills, &c.

In addition to the distinguished honour Mr. Robins had of being introduced to Her Majesty at Osborne, I.W., 16th August, 1878, he received her royal command and painted for her the *Wreck of H.M.S. "Eurydice,"* lying in Sandown Bay, I.W., also the *Naval Review at Spithead, 13th August, 1878.*

OSBORNE, August 16th, 1878.

Lieut.-General Ponsonby is commanded by the Queen to state that Her Majesty is much pleased with the sketch of the Naval Review executed by Mr. Robins.

WINDSOR CASTLE, 21st March, 1883.

Sir Henry Ponsonby has to inform Mr. Robins that the Queen has seen his two pictures, and will be glad to purchase the small one, "'Landing of the Scots Guards.''

Subsequently the Queen purchased Mr. Robin's picture of the "Landing of the Scots Guards" at Portsmouth, on their arrival from Egypt, 15th November, 1882; which now hangs in the Grand Corridor at Windsor Castle.

Lessons given in Marine Painting

EITHER AT HIS STUDIO OR PRIVATELY.

Henry Robins' advertisement headed by the royal coat of arms and the crests of Queen Victoria and the Prince of Wales.

funeral.[13] When Grandpa Robins was commissioned as artist for the Royal Families, he became Sir Henry Robins. He married a titled lady from France, Lady Jane Proux of Cherbourg and same title for England.[14]

They had thirteen children. My mother was the youngest and Lady Jane died when my mother was four years old.

Grandpa raised his children solely by making each older one take care of the next one in line and he supervised them all as to habits – dress, school, etc. The crest of the mailed fist was handed down to the family from another relative of the Robins family, a Sir Henry Robins at the Battles of Portieres and Crecy, France in 1346. This former Robins was in service under the Black Prince, who was the son of King Edward III, so called by black uniforms he wore. Robins was in a bather (toilet to us) and heard of a plan to kill the Prince. Right away he hurried to his superiors not waiting to fix his attire and was held for his unmanly appearance. Soon he was able to explain to their satisfaction and the attempted plot was stopped.

Citations and crest and titles have been carried down through the years. So Grandpa's title was really double. When Grandpa – Sir Henry – was painting for royalty, the Queen's son, the Prince of Wales, allowed him to use the crest 'Ich Dien', which is held by every Prince of Wales since 1346 to be used on home and business papers.

The crest of the iron mailed fist can be used on carriages, door entrances, silverware and stationery. The crest came to England in the time of the war with France. It was the crest of the King of Bohemia whose troops were helping the French in their battle in 1346. He was noted as a gallant fighter of all countries and always led his men in battle. However, the King was now blind and ordered his men to fasten his horse between two others and lead him into the battle. The Black Prince hearing of this planned to make him a prisoner but he was too late. He found him dead, his sightless eyes turned to the skies and his helmet beside him, holding the Crest of the three feathers.

[13] *Duke of Wellington's funeral 1852.*

[14] *Henry Robins is recorded as marrying Susannah Jane Prouw 16th September 1846.*

Henry Robins on his 70th birthday. © B Huntsinger

At first the Black Prince paid homage to such a great fighter and then took the crest for a tribute. Later he placed it for the crest of all Princes of Wales that would come down in the line.[15] England is still holding that crest today. The sign of the three feathers 'Ich Dien', which means 'I serve'.

Robins' inventions

Grandpa was very clever with machinery and had several inventions under way. He was the first inventor of the Mittrailleuse Gatling Nordenfeldt guns. See *United Service Gazette* 1861, 1870; also *Hampshire Telegraph* 1880.

The first man to accomplish a Daguerreotype picture in England.

He also wrote a book called 'Joe the Marine, ashore and afloat', which was taken down in writing by a war correspondent then put aside for years, when Mother asked me to put it all down in book form.

This I have done taking six months of steady writing and then had Flo my sister type it up. It is written around his life and war experiences with many funny anecdotes and it is well worth reading, but he preferred to call it 'Joe the Marine'.

[15] *Considered to be a myth.*

Aunt Laura

One of Mother's sisters, Aunt Laura[16], married Captain Jack Usmar whose mother was a Countess and at one time owned the Island of Coll.[17] The Isle used to be called Caul. They lived on the island for a while and then the Army called and they were shipped to India, where they spent many years. Aunt Laura was a very beautiful woman and artists painted her many times.

An Indian prince was so pleased with her painting he requested an interview with her. Uncle Jack with some of his men escorted her and had a very nice visit. Later a jewelled casket was delivered by the prince's men with many gifts inside and instructions to pick out what she would like to keep as a memento of her visit.

Aunt Laura returned the casket saying all was so beautiful and hard to choose but as she was a regimental man's wife she would have to return them. Back came the casket with word it was a complimentary gift and with her captain's approval she should accept them. The Captain approved and the jewels, later sent to my mother, was shared by sister Flo and myself. Now at 92 years I am passing some of it along to my grandchildren and telling them how we received them.

Among my souvenirs is also a Coronation mug I received at the Coronation of Queen Alexandra and King Edward in 1902.

My sister and I had been invited to the Coronation and was asked to meet the Princess of Battenberg and her attendants as she arrived by train. We met Princess Beatrice with our arms full of flowers from Hill Lodge.

---

[16] *George 'Jack' Alleyne Usmar b. 1851 is recorded as marring Eliza Jane Robins, another of Nell's aunts. Serving in the Royal Artillery, mostly in India, Jack returned to the UK after Eliza's death in Lucknow in 1887, and was resident with his five children in Campbeltown, Scotland at the time of the 1891 census. In 1919 at age 69 Jack emigrated to Barbados.*
[17] *Located West of Mull, Inner Hebrides.*

Laura Robins. © B Huntsinger

The Princess was so pleased she put a medal of Princess Beatrice around my neck and gave my sister Ada coins of her country as a memento of the occasion.

Later all gathered on a wide lawn to rest, served tea in Royal cups and told to keep them. I did and have now passed them on to my son. The cup has the King and Queen's portrait on them, the Royal Crest and date 1902.

My brother was also given the courteous invitation at the next Coronation and also received a cup with portraits of Queen Mary and King George 22nd June 1911. This cup is also held by my son, Louis Arthur Bruggeman, born 1924 to Ellen Stevenson and William Bruggemann.

Louis Arthur Bruggeman

Louis Arthur Bruggeman married Elinor Margaret Vaill 4th June 1951. Two children were born to them, Rick Vaill and Victoria Jane Bruggeman. Rick married Julie Mills 2nd August 1975 and has two children, Amanda Jeanne and Daniel Ryan Bruggeman.

Victoria married John Knopf in 1974 and they have three children, Genesis Dawn, Kari Adell and David John.

Coronation mug 1902.

Coronation mug 1911.

Coronation programme 1902.

Post script

When I was about twelve years old we got in touch with a Reverend Robins just assigned to our Church. On visiting our home he was so surprised to see Grandpa's portrait on the wall and some of his paintings. 'Why', he said, 'you have my Uncle Henry's pictures here.' Then we learned that the Reverend and my mother were cousins.

He and other of the Robins ancestors had gone thru the history of the Robins line and had traced them back for 400 years to the fact that the eldest of each family had been a soldier or a marine in their time. Mother was delighted and was also promised a copy of the books but before Mother got them he died of cancer and no one knows what became of those copies. At least that was what Mother was told. I remember him saying it went back to the time when an ancestor had been knighted for saving the life of the Black Prince. He was given the title Sir Henry Robins to be carried down thru the family line. Those missing papers, I am sure, would have been good reading.

I trust these writings will be passed on to my family.
Ellen Victoria Jane Stevenson Bruggemann Ventresca

Family Notes

These family notes have been compiled from information from living relatives with online research.

Ada Robins Stevenson

Ada Robins Stevenson's distress over her husband's philandering can only be imagined and might have broken some families, but Ada was not to be bested. Having made the brave decision to reunite her family, she suffered badly with seasickness aboard SS *City of New York* before stepping onto American soil with thirteen-year-old Florence and eleven-year-old Christopher, on 19th May 1912.

Referred to as 'ahead of her time' and 'a strong, gutsy and powerful woman with a lusty sense of humour', who expressed her thoughts on women's rights freely in the press, Ada lived to become the wife

Ada Maria Robins Stevenson.

Ada & Edward Bedbrook. © V Knopf

of three times Mayor of Montreal Edward Bedbrook, and to see Flo and Christopher grow to adulthood. Would any of them have survived had she not had her dreadful premonition about *Titanic* and cancelled their passage?

Ada felt her ability to foresee bad events, such as the death of friends, to be a curse rather than a blessing and would dearly have liked sometimes to see good things. Bidding 'Goodbye old house for I shall never see you again' when driven to hospital, what was perhaps Ada's final premonition proved sadly to be accurate. Ada Robins Stevenson Bedbrook passed away in Waterbury, Connecticut in 1946 aged 80.

Obituary of Ada Maria Robins Stevenson Bedbrook.

Ada Margaret 'Maggie' Stevenson

Ada Margaret 'Maggie' Stevenson married Carman Perugini and gave birth to two children, Angelina Florence and George Robins Perugini.

However, finding parenthood difficult, Maggie allowed Lena and George to be fostered by Flo for several years during the Great Depression of the 1930s.

Referred to by Nell as 'the rock of the entire family', Flo took care of EVERYBODY at one time or other.

Ada 'Maggie' Perugini passed away in Southgate, California in 1971.

Ada Margaret 'Maggie' Stevenson.
© V Knopf

Angelina Florence Perugini.
© V Knopf

Angelina Florence Perugini Turello

Angelina Florence Perugini Turello passed away in Los Angeles in January 1955 aged 36.

George Perugini

George Perugini passed away in California in July 1988 aged 67; his son Carman was no doubt named after George's father.

Florence Georgina Geraldine Stevenson

Florence Georgina Geraldine Stevenson, an accomplished pianist, joined the Musicians' Union and worked in Waterbury theatres to help support her family from the tender age of fourteen. Accompanying silent films and Vaudeville, the shy young English girl was dismayed to find elderly gentlemen in jockstraps – Vaudeville performers – playing poker in theatre basements, but, encouraged to 'ignore them honey, just go get the music', she proceeded to play the pump organ with enthusiasm as cowboys, Indians and cavalry chased across the plains.

Florence Georgina Geraldine Stevenson. © B Huntsinger

In 1926 Mae West's self-penned show 'Sex' was tried out in Waterbury before opening on Broadway. When sent to 'report back with the story', Flo's verdict of 'funny, but vulgar' was borne out less than a year later with the play closed and Mae charged with 'corrupting the morals of youth'.

Sentenced to ten days in the Women's Workhouse on Welfare Island (now Roosevelt Island), Mae is said to have dined with and entertained the Governor and his wife for eight days, before being released with two days off for 'good behaviour'.

Flo continued to work in theatres following her marriage to Romeo

Mae West's scandalous show.

Carosello while Ada looked after the home and later cared for Robert, born 1924, and Barbara, born six years later in 1930, joined during the Great Depression by Maggie's children George and Angelina.

Widowed by Romeo's death in 1969, it wasn't until shortly before her own death, twenty years later, that, shaking and in tears, Flo unburdened herself of a lifelong secret that had perhaps contributed to Maggie's difficulties in raising her children – that of Maggie's schoolgirl pregnancy. Nell and Maggie were both at St Joseph's School at this time when, to provide an innocent explanation for Maggie's increasing girth, Nell was made to dress with pillows under her clothing to give the impression that the two girls were both gaining weight in the fresh country air. Sadly Maggie's infant didn't survive, which may account for there being no apparent record of this event.

The 'Little Peace Maker' of Hill Lodge, baptized by Dr Joseph Merriman in All Saints' Parish Church, Freshwater on 6th August 1899, lived on to welcome great-grandchildren Steven in 1970, Cindi in 1972, David in 1983 and Erin in 1985 to her family before passing away in Los Angeles, California in 1988, aged 89 and still with British citizenship.

Robert Carosello

Robert & Christine Carosello c1989.

Robert Carosello's childhood days in Connecticut were followed by teenage years in wartime France where, working on tanks and military vehicles, he learned skills in mechanics that were to last his lifetime.

Returning home at the end of the war, Robert married Christine Sorvillo and they settled in Downey, California. Following the sad loss of three-year-old Steven in 1951, daughters Paula and Karen were born in 1953 and 1955 to be

60

raised in the 'Golden State' during the idyllic sixties, while Bob ran a successful auto-parts store in Costa Mesa before moving in later years to Banning, California.

Paula and Karen, now with Karen's children Steven and Cindi and grandchildren Emily Grace, Jaden, Lauren and Brennan, continue to visit Christine in Banning since Bob passed away in 2014 aged 89.

Barbara Jean Carosello Luedeka

Barbara Jean Carosello Luedeka combined caring for her mother Flo in her Norwalk home with the long commute to her work in the office of Michelin Tire.

After Flo's death, Barb moved to Ontario, where in 1991 her life and that of a colleague were saved by seatbelts in a horrific freeway collision, although they suffered massive bruising and multiple fractures. Accepting early retirement shortly afterwards, life should have become easier for Barb, but sadly grief had not yet done with her; in

Barbara & William Luedeka Snr.
© B Huntsinger

1992, the day following his discharge from hospital, her eldest child, Bill, passed away aged 38 in his Long Beach apartment. Affectionately remembered by his family as 'enterprising and a little eccentric', Bill, who changed his name to Matthew Greg Miller simply because the initials MGM appealed to him, had published the *Long Beach Community Newspaper*. Following the shock of Greg's death, Barb moved closer to her daughter Bonnie, in Nashville.

Ellen Victoria Jane Stevenson

Ellen nee Stevenson. © V Knopf

Nell's handiwork.

Nicholas & Nell Ventresca.

Ellen Victoria Jane Stevenson's health problems led to short-term jobs ranging from furrier, seamstress and waitress to producing bows for Helene Curtis cosmetics, assembling hat boxes, and the application of luminous paint to watch and clock faces. Bringing brushes to a fine point with lips and tongue, Nell became one of thousands to be known as 'radium girls' with teeth and skin that glowed, and jaw problems found many years later to be caused by toxic radium in the paint.

In 1924, during her short marriage to William Bruggemann, Nell's only child, Louis Arthur, was born. As he grew up, the young Louis found he could get away with very little, as his mother had clearly inherited Ada's sixth sense and usually knew what he'd been up to before he arrived home. That sense was still apparent many years later when, unknown to Nell, one of her great-grandchildren went 'walkabout' for several hours at age twelve. Wailing that 'the children are missing, the children are missing', it wasn't until the child had safely returned that Nell could be calmed.

With much of her time spent with her great-nieces in Norwalk, Nell shared the skills learned at Freshwater School, so that beautiful handmade items have been passed down through her family.

Marrying again in 1958, Nell and second husband Nicholas Ventresca lived happily in their bungalow until Nick's death in the 1970s. Nell then lived alone until, fitted with a pacemaker and now a little unsteady on her feet, she lay unseen in the garden for several hours after a fall. With Flo insisting that Nell should now move in to share her home, Barbara kept a caring eye on her mother and aunt while her daughters Bonnie and Val enjoyed chatting and sharing meals with the sisters and sometimes persuaded Flo to play the organ to an audience of school friends.

However, in 1984 disaster struck when Flo too had a fall. Joining Louis and Elinor in Medina, Ohio, Nell was devastated when just eight months later Elinor passed away, so that after a short stay in hospital she decided to move into nursing care. Here she made new friends, enjoyed visits and trips with Vicki and witnessed great-grandson David's first steps, taken among residents and walking canes.

With Jonathan born to Genesis in 1991, Nell became a great-great-grandmother at age 99; a good-looking and popular lad, Jonathan's life was tragically cut short in an automobile accident in 2012, while Genesis and Amer's younger children, Angeline, Adam, Aaron, Mickell and Riyan, were never to meet their great-great-grandmother. Ellen Victoria Jane Stevenson Bruggemann Ventresca passed away in 1992, four months after her 100th birthday.

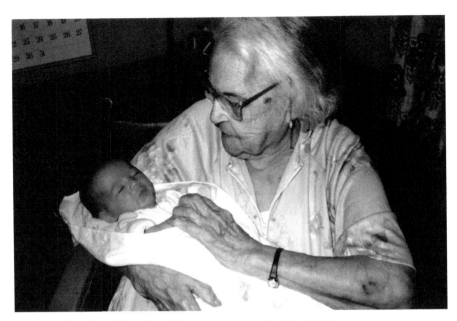

Jonathan cradled in the arms of Great-great-grandmother Nell.

100th birthday celebration napkin.

I wonder why...

I hear voices and there's no one there,
I see mother in her favourite chair,
I hear Bob, and Louis starts to cry
I wonder why...I wonder why?

I see pastures that are never green,
I hear laughter that is never seen
I see kind folks turn so very mean
I wonder why...I wonder why?

I go walking down the street
see unborn children I have yet to meet,
the mother's smile makes it all worthwhile
I wonder why...I wonder why?

Ellen Victoria Jane Bruggemann

Louis Bruggeman

Louis Bruggeman. © V Knopf

Louis Bruggeman (who dropped the final 'n' in his surname) loved animals, and became a skilled horseman and prize-winning dog breeder with many trophies.

Marriage to Elinor Vaill in Waterbury, Connecticut in 1951 was followed by a honeymoon in California, where they settled and were later joined by both sets of parents. With Rick's birth in 1952 followed by Victoria's in 1955, Louis and Elinor's family was complete.

Moving on to Utah in the late 1950s, Louis travelled through several states as construction machinery salesman for JI Case, and won the title 'Salesman of the year' before a second move, to Indiana, in 1970.

Four years later when their parents moved once more, to establish a real estate business in Ohio, Rick and Vicki remained in Indiana where they each later married.

Widowed by Elinor's death in 1985, Louis retired from the real estate business in 1989 to enjoy painting, crafting and his role of Drum Major in bagpipe bands.

Finding happiness again, he married Barbara Miller in 1987 when Nell gained a second daughter-in-law who was to become a dear friend.

Following Louis' death in 2005 aged 81, Barbara spent time with her eldest daughter in Texas then settled close to her younger daughter in Mt Juliet, Tennessee, where her family visit regularly.

Louis and Elinor Bruggeman.   Drum Major Louis Bruggeman.

Barbara & Louis Bruggeman 1987.

Richard Henry Stevenson

Richard Henry Stevenson is recorded as being treated at Makina Masus for sandfly fever in June 1916 and then being transferred to Mohammerah Convalescent hospital in July 1917. It is thought that he returned to the UK from Jubbulpore for discharge from Military Service in May 1920. Richard's medals are recorded as being returned to the Medal Office.

Richard Stevenson c1910.

Christopher William Stevenson

Christopher William Stevenson, baptised in All Saints' Parish Church, Freshwater on 11th August 1901, grew up in the United States from age eleven. Chris left Waterbury for Canada in the 1940s where, before losing contact with his family, he was photographed with his son. Despite years of searching, Nell was never to hear more of either of her brothers.

Christopher Stevenson with son.
© B Huntsinger

68

Colours, 18th Battn. Irish Regiment of Foot.

Parkhurst Military Cemetery,
Isle of Wight. © Geoff Allan

William James Stevenson

Born in Sligo, Portadown, Co. Armagh in 1852, William James
Stevenson enlisted in the 1st Battalion 18th (The Royal Irish)
Regiment of Foot on 13th October 1870. Private 2040 Stevenson's
Attestation papers state that a weaver of height 5' 7½", William had a
fresh complexion, grey eyes and brown hair and was of 'slight' build.
Serving in Malta, India, Afghanistan and Egypt, William was
awarded The Afghan Campaign Medal 1878–80, Egyptian medal
with clasp Nile Expedition 1884–85, and Khedive Bronze Star 1884.
Discharged in April 1892 having completed 21½ years' service, 2040
Colour Sergeant William Stevenson served as a Barrack Warden on
the Isle of Wight until his death in 1910. William's grave in Parkhurst
Military Cemetery, Isle of Wight is one of many sadly no longer
marked[18].

[18] *Research suggests that William's visit to Bournemouth to see 'the first planes in England'
might have been to the Bournemouth Aviation Week in July 1910 and that the storm that
drenched him, leading to his demise, was that which forced actor/aviator Robert Loraine to crash
land on the Alum Bay Golf Course, the first aircraft to land on the Isle of Wight.*

DEATH OF BARRACK WARDEN STEVENSON.—The death occurred at Carisbrooke on Friday last, after a long and painful illness, of Barrack Warden William James Stevenson, who was well known and greatly respected here by both soldiers and civilians. The late Mr. Stevenson had been barrack warden at Fort Victoria for the past 16 years and until just recently resided at Hill Lodge, Norton. A little more than a month ago he went on an excursion to Bournemouth with his fellow N.C. officers and caught a severe chill which developed into chronic pneumonia and complications from which he died. Mr. Stevenson was formerly in the 18th Royal Irish Regiment. He went through both the Afghan and Egyptian (Gordon Relief) campaigns and received the medal and medal and star for them. He was also awarded the long service and good conduct medal. The deceased was a stanch Conservative and for several years was an able hon. treasurer of the Freshwater Conservative Club. His loss will be widely mourned and the deepest sympathy is felt for his wife and five children. His age was 57. The funeral took place with military honours at the Military Cemetery, Parkhurst, on Wednesday, in the presence of many friends from the west of the Island. Those present included Capt. Maloney, A.S.C., Lieut. Bizzett and a party of N.C. officers and men from the 22 Co. R.E., Fort Victoria, several staff sergeants and N.C. officers of the R.G.A. from Golden Hill, Messrs. W. J. Elliott, W. and M. Reason, and S. E. R. Nicholls. The firing party was composed of men of the 2nd Suffolks, whilst the barrack wardens of the Island acted as bearers. The Rev. S. P. H. Statham officiated. There were a large number of wreaths, including those from his wife and family, Mr. and Mrs. W. J. Elliott, Mr. and Mrs. Tanner, the R.E. office, the staff sergeants and sergeants of the Royal Engineers (Fort Victoria), the barrack wardens, and the sergeants' mess, Golden Hill. Messrs. H. and F. Damp, of Newport, carried out the funeral arrangements.

Obituary for William James Stevenson, *Isle of Wight County Press* 27th August 1910.

RECORD OF SERVICE.

W. O. Form 497.

No. **1254** Name **William James Stevenson**

Joined at

on **2 MAY 92** CHELSEA

B

PROCEEDINGS ON ATTESTATION

Six Years Army Service and Six Years Army Reserve. (1st Class) Service.

Questions to be put to the Recruit before Attestation.

Richard Airey A.G.

1. What is your Name? — **William James Stevenson**
2. In what Parish, and in or near what Town, and in what County were you born? — In the Parish of **Seago** in or near the Town of **Portadown** in the County of **Armagh**
3. What is your Age? — **18** Years **6** Months.
4. What is your Trade or Calling? — **Weaver**
5. Are you an Apprentice? — **No**
6. Are you Married? — **No**
7. Do you now belong to the Militia, or Army or Militia Reserve, or to the Naval Coast Volunteers? or to the Royal Naval Reserve Force? ... — **No**
   Do you belong to any Regiment, Brigade or Corps in Her Majesty's Army? — **No**
8. Have you ever served in the Army, Marines, Militia, or Navy? ... — **No**
   If so, the Recruit is to state the particulars of his former Service, and the cause of his Discharge, and is to produce his Parchment Certificate of Discharge.
9. Have you ever been rejected as unfit for Her Majesty's Service, upon any prior Enlistment? — **No**
10. Have you ever been marked with the letter "D" or the letters "B C"? — **No**
11. Where, when, by whom, and for what Regiment, Brigade or Corps, were you enlisted, or were you enlisted for General Service? — For* At **Lurgan** on the **13** day of **Oct** 18**70** at **10** o'Clock, A. M. By **Sergt Robert Sterling Pension Recruiting 1st Staff**
12. Did you receive a Notice, and did you understand its meaning? — **Yes**
13. For what Bounty and Kit did you enlist? — **No Bounty but** a free Kit.
14. Have you any objection to make to the manner of your enlistment? — **No**
15. Are you willing to be attested to serve for the term of twelve Years, provided Her Majesty should so long require your services? — **Yes**
16. Are you willing to serve for a further term of twelve months if abroad, or if a state of War exists between Her Majesty and any Foreign power, if you should be ordered so to serve by the Secretary of State for War, or by the Commanding Officer on any Foreign, Colonial, or Indian Station? — **Yes**

Do you understand that during the term of your Service in the Army, you are liable to be called upon to serve in any Regiment of the Army by Her Majesty's permission in time of imminent national danger or of great emergency?

Signature of Recruit **(Sd) Wm Jas + Stevenson**
mark

Witness **(Sd) Fred N Magahan**

DECLARATION TO BE MADE BY RECRUIT ON ATTESTATION.

I, do solemnly and sincerely declare, That to the best of my Knowledge and Belief the above answers to the foregoing questions made and signed by me, are true; and that I am willing to be attested for the Term of Twelve Years provided Her Majesty should so long require my Services, and also, if abroad, or if a state of War exists between Her Majesty and any Foreign Power, for any further term, not exceeding Twelve Months, as shall be directed by the Secretary of State for War, or the Commanding Officer on any Foreign, Colonial, or Indian Station.

(Sd) Wm Jas his mark Stevenson Signature of Recruit

(Sd) Fred W Magahan Signature of Witness

OATH TO BE TAKEN BY RECRUIT ON ATTESTATION.

I, **Wm Jas Stevenson** do make Oath, that I will be faithful and bear true Allegiance to Her Majesty, Her Heirs, and Successors, and that I will, as in duty bound, honestly and faithfully defend Her Majesty, Her Heirs, and Successors, in Person, Crown, and Dignity, against all enemies, and will observe and obey all orders of Her Majesty, Her Heirs, and Successors, and of the Generals and Officers set over me. So help me God.

Witness my hand.

Signature of Recruit **(Sd) Wm Jas mark Stevenson**
Witness present **(Sd) Fred W Magahan**

The above questions were asked of the said **Wm Jas Stevenson** and answered by him in my presence, as herein recorded; and the said **Wm Jas Stevenson** made the above Declaration and Oath before me at **Lurgan** this **14** day of **October** One Thousand eight hundred and **Seventy** at **11 20** o'Clock, A.M.

Signature of the Justice **(Sd) James A Bell**

* Here insert the particular Regiment, Sub-District Brigade, or Corps for which the man was enlisted. In the case of a Recruit enlisted for General Service, the words "General Service" will be inserted.

Enlistment 13th October 1870.

STATEMENT of the SERVICES of No. 1784 Name William James Stevenson

Corps in which served	Battn. or Depot	Promotions, Reductions, Casualties, &c.	Army Rank	Dates	Service not allowed to reckon for fixing the rate of Pension		Service in Reserve not allowed to reckon towards G. C. Pay.		Signature of Officer certifying correctness of Entries
					years	days	years	days	
		Service towards limited engagement reckons from 4 Oct 1871							
The R.S.Reg Depot		Posted	C/Sergt	1st April 87					Stan Michaelis Coff Col
"	"	Permitted to continue in the Service, beyond 21 years. in accordance with Sec: 85 a. act. 1881	"	6. 10. 91					W. Smith Adjutant 18th Regimental District.
"	"	Granted 5d. G. C. Pay. 14.10.91 (had he not been promoted)							W. Smith Captain Adjutant 18th Regimental District
"	"	Discharged	C/Sergt	30. 4. 92					R. Smith Capt Captain Adjutant 18th Regimental District

Total amount of Service forfeited towards pension, and not allowed to reckon towards G. C. Pay brought forward from the old Record ...			Nil	Nil
Total Service forfeited as above			Nil	Nil
Total Service towards Engagement to **30.4.92** (date of discharge)			**21** years **200** days	

Certified by W. Smith. Major
Commanding Depot Royal Irish Re

F A T 100,000 5—88

Discharge 30th April 1892.

The Graphic 12th June 1886 A NILE TROPHY

When the recent Nile Expedition was organised, Lord Wolseley offered a prize of £100 to the regiment which should perform the journey up the river in the whale-boats from Sarras to Debbah in the shortest time and with the fewest accidents. The prize was won by the 1st Battalion of the Royal Irish Regiment in the face of considerable difficulties, while the regiment subsequently added to its laurels by a march across the Bayuda Desert from Korti to Metemmeh, the Royal Irish being the only regiment which, up to that time, had performed the journey on foot. On the prize being awarded, it became a matter of difficulty to decide how the money could be best laid out so as to give satisfaction to all who had taken part in the hard task of winning it. It was ultimately settled that it should be invested in a piece of plate, which would always remain in the regiment as a memento of the event.

The work of producing a suitable piece of plate was undertaken by Messrs. Stephen Smith and Sons, King Street, Covent Garden and was carried out to the entire satisfaction of all concerned.

The trophy represents a whaler-boat in full sail, complete with oars, boat-hooks, tow-lines, &c, all in solid silver, sailing on a sea of silver, and is mounted on a pedestal of ebony, which, on a silver shield, bears a copy of the following letter which accompanied Lord Wolseley's cheque:

Camp Korti, 11th March 1885

Dear Colonel Shaw

It is with the greatest pleasure I send you the enclosed cheque for £100, the prize won by your splendid battalion by having gone up the Nile to Debbah in boats in less time than any other regiment. Being an Irishman myself, it is very gratifying to feel that my small prize has been carried off by my own countrymen.

Believe me to be, dear Col. Shaw,

Very truly yours, Wolesley.

The Nile trophy from *The Graphic* 12th June 1886.

On the other side is the motto of the regiment. The ends of the pedestal are enriched with representations in silver of the troops hauling boats up the Cataracts, and the Desert Column marching en route to Metemmeh.

The engraving is from a photograph by Mr John Hawke, 8 George Street, Plymouth.

Cheney Velvet Mill

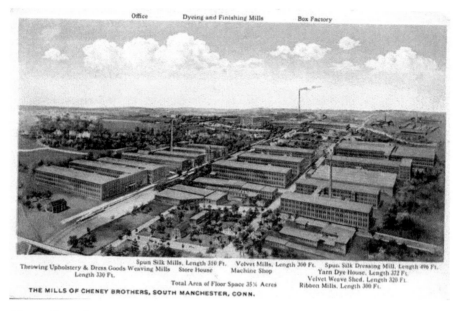

THE MILLS OF CHENEY BROTHERS, SOUTH MANCHESTER, CONN.

Cheney Bros. Company Town.

Cheney Velvet Mill formed part of Cheney Brothers Company Town in South Manchester, Connecticut where housing, schools, libraries, theatres and churches stood among mills and Cheney family mansions.

Many thousands of employees could walk to work to produce fine silk, velvet and ribbon while the Cheney South Manchester Railway provided both commercial and passenger transport.

With mills and mansions now largely converted to apartments and offices, the area was declared a National History Landmark in 1978.

The Old Ship Vane on St Thomas's Church, Portsmouth

Old ship you've swung a hundred years and many more besides,
the bells have rung for victory gained, gay weddings, Christmas tide
and oft' they've toll'd in solemn sound for warriors great, and kings,
you've floated high above them all in the belfry where they swing.

You've stood the storm, the heat and cold as on spire top you sit,
there's not an emblem to be found, not one could be fit.
Pray Heaven protect that secret pile that stands beneath your kiel,
long may you float in tranquil air, long may the old bells peal.

Then thunders roll and lightning flash and storms sweep o'er the sea,
bold mariners with eager eyes look anxiously for thee
and bring to them thy joyous bells
so dear to them and me.

Henry Robins

Hampshire Telegraph & Sussex Chronicle
23rd August 1873

The ship on the tower of St Thomas's Church, Portsmouth was raised again to its position on Monday after being re-gilded by Mr Gray, of Point. By a date on its deck it is shown that the ship was made of copper in the year 1710 and was re-gilt on the 17th August 1842. It also bears the names of:

JP McGie, Vicar; TJ Brown, Curate; CH Binsteed and J Holmes, Churchwardens.

The dimensions of the ship are: Extreme length 6ft 10in; length of hull 3ft 5in; and length from keel to top of mainmast 4ft 2in. Mr Henry Robins of Landport has taken a beautiful photograph of the ship, with portraits of the Vicar and Churchwardens in the background.

Ship weather vane on top of St Thomas's Church, now Portsmouth Cathedral.
© Bryan Moffatt 2016

The Wreck of the "Eurydice". Signed and dated by Henry Robins on 9th August 1878.

Royal Collection Trust © Her Majesty Queen Elizabeth II 2016.

HMS *Eurydice* was a training ship that sank off Sandown Bay, Isle of Wight in a sudden squall on 24th March 1878. Of more than 300 men on board, there were just two survivors. In the painting, the ship is being pumped out below Culver Cliff before removal to Portsmouth Harbour.

Hampshire Telegraph
24th August 1878

Mr Robins, marine artist, of Commercial Road, Landport, has completed a large oil painting representing the operations in connection with the raising of the *Eurydice* in Sandown Bay. The picture shows the wreck, together with the *Pearl, Rinaldo, Wave, Swan,* the steam tugs &c., and is very complete in every detail. Mr Robins has also executed a capital sketch of the naval inspection at Spithead by the Queen. The artist had the honour of submitting both works personally to the inspection of Her Majesty at Osborne on Thursday, when she expressed herself highly pleased with them and purchased a copy of the first-named picture together with the sketch. Mr Robins also had the honour of showing the pictures to HRH the Prince of Wales, who also expressed his satisfaction. A singular fact in connection with the picture is that it was painted in less than forty hours. Mr Robins is a retired sergeant from the Royal Marine Artillery and claims to have been the inventor of the mitrailleuse.

Hampshire Telegraph
3rd September 1887

Singular Coincidence—The daughter of Mr Henry Robins, marine artist of 11 Norfolk Square, Southsea, died somewhat suddenly at the residence of her father on the 31st of July. On Wednesday Mr Robins received an intimation that his other daughter, the wife of BS Major Usmar, Royal Artillery, died suddenly from fatty degeneration of the heart at Ranikhet on the 1st of August. Both, it seems, were buried on the same day, and so far as can be ascertained, precisely at the same hour.

Hampshire Advertiser 18th February 1880

THE NORDËNFELDT GUN A LOCAL INVENTION—It will be remembered by many of our local readers who take an interest in matters affecting the Services that the principle of the mitrailleuse, a weapon used with such deadly effect during the Franco-German struggle, originated with Mr Henry Robins, marine artist, residing in Commercial Road, who was for many years connected with the Royal Marine Artillery, in which Corps he attained the rank of Provost Sergeant. Mr Robins invented a weapon upon the principle in question as far back as 1858, and submitted a model with carriage, scale 1in. to the foot, to the War Office, who sent it before the Ordnance Select Committee in 1859, but it was returned with a statement "that it was of no use" or words to that effect, although it was the opinion of many who saw it that it was a weapon of great execution, and that it would eventually be used in warfare. Mr Robins

Nordenfeldt gun. Image courtesy of Australian Army Infantry Museum.

being in London in 1861 went to the Patent Office in Trafalgar Square, and had an interview with Mr Prince with respect to his 'compound breech-loading rifle', the name given to it by the Ordnance Select Committee. That gentleman informed him that a foreign officer was in London in search of something new, and as the English Government had rejected it, it might turn out to his advantage to show it to him. This was agreed to, and Mr Prince paid Mr Robins' expenses to Portsmouth to bring up the model which was shown to the foreign gentleman in Trafalgar Square, who, through Mr Prince, made every inquiry of the inventor. The 'foreign gentleman' was no doubt the 'inventor' who subsequently introduced the mitrailleuse into the French Army.

It will be seen that Mr Robins had been allowed to drop into the official Lethe of un-patronised genius, and never from that day to this has he received the slightest recognition. We mentioned these circumstances at the time, and only repeat them after all these years because in the Nordenfeldt weapon, which is now upon its trial and about which so much has been said and written, we recognise even in a stronger degree than the mitrailleuse Provost-Sergeant Robins' invention. We have before us an old photograph of Mr Robins' working model taken in 1858, and comparing this with the descriptions which have appeared of the Nordenfeldt gun it is clear to see that the latter only differs in some of its details.

Mr Robins' model shows the barrels fixed in parallel form (an arrangement that the Nordenfeldt claims to be superior to the rotary arrangement of the Gatling gun), while in the Nordenfeldt gun for use on shore the arrangements for limbering &c., are precisely similar to those of the model referred to. Surely, if the whole of the circumstances were fairly represented to the authorities whose province it is to deal with such matters, an old veteran who, we are assured, spent a large sum of money and several months of anxious labour in producing the invention which he unsuccessfully submitted, will not be passed over without some sort of recognition, if only as an incentive to other men with brains to work for the improvement of the weapons of our own Service.

Stevenson family minus Richard. Hill Lodge, Freshwater c1902. From left: William Stevenson, Florence, Ellen, Maggie, Ada holding baby Christopher, two servants. © B Huntsinger

Hill Lodge, Freshwater c2015.

Meet of IW hounds, Yarmouth, 12th February 1909. Wm Stevenson mounted far right.

Meet of IW hounds, Yarmouth, 12th February 1909. Wm Stevenson mounted far right.

Extracts from report in *Freshwater, Totland and Yarmouth Advertiser* Friday 19th April 1912

Farewell Concert at Freshwater

... There was a fairly good audience at the farewell concert arranged by Mrs Ada Stevenson at the Assembly Rooms on Wednesday evening. Mrs Stevenson, when formerly living at Freshwater, was always one of the foremost to lend her aid to any deserving cause and as she is leaving the Island to reside with her two daughters abroad, the occasion was taken by a few useful friends to organise the concert on her behalf...

... Miss F. Stevenson, who showed considerable promise for so young a vocalist and has an excellent voice, sang 'In the city where nobody cares' with really astonishing purity and clearness; the talented young lady fully deserved her encore and her response song 'Meet me in Dreamland' was equally as good...

... Mrs Ada Stevenson, whose voice appears to have lost none of its old charm and tone, gave two pleasing items, and was enthusiastically re-demanded, giving the popular and appropriate song 'Off to Philadelphia.' She was also the recipient of a handsome bouquet for which she bowed her acknowledgements and thanks. The whole programme was a credit to both the organisers and artistes, and 'The King' concluded a highly appreciated programme...

Sources

Ancestry www.ancestry.co.uk

Argyll and Bute Council Archives www.argyll-bute.gov.uk

Australian Army Infantry Museum www.australianmuseum.net.au

British Newspaper Archive www.britishnewspaperarchive.co.uk

Findmypast www.findmypast.co.uk

Forces War Records www.forces-war-records.co.uk

Herefordshire Past www.herefordshirepast.co.uk

Isle of Wight County Press http://archive.iwcp.co.uk

IW County Record Office www.iwight.com/council/Record Office

'Joe the Marine, ashore and afloat' Henry Robins

Manchester Historical Society www.manchesterhistory.org

The British Empire www.britishempire.co.uk

The National Archives www.nationalarchives.gov.uk

The Royal Artillery Museum www.armymuseums.org.uk

The Royal Collection Trust www.royalcollection.org.uk

Waterbury Observer, September 2002